MW01489934

A 2007 eruptive column at Mount Etna producing volcanic ash, pumice and lava bombs

Mt Fuji Volcano Foggy Mountain Mount Fuji

Hawaii Volcano Hot Fire Night Evening Flames

New Zealand Volcano Crater White Island Island

Geology Volcano Crater Haleakala Landscape

Volcano Crater Lava Glow Hot Geology Silhouette

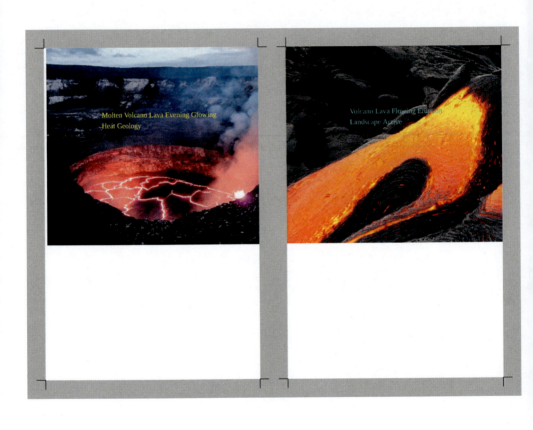

Dawn Desert Fog Geology Lake Landscape Mountain

Piton Caribbean Volcano Pitons Landscape

Merapi Mountain Indonesia Volcano Java Outdoor

Algeria Hoggar Assekrem Volcano Erosion Desert

Japan Aso Kumamoto Cloud Volcano Light Asahi Sky

Popocatepetl Mexico Volcano Mexican Landscape

Magma Lava Volcano Volcanism
Guatemala Liquid

Planet Alien Sky Star
Galaxy Ring Space
Universe

Volcano Java Indonesia Mount Seremu
Mount Merapi

Iceland Mountain Volcano Landscape

Volcano Halemaʻumaʻu Lava Lake Sunset

Iceland Crater Volcano Lake

Volcano Geography Views Indonesia Steam

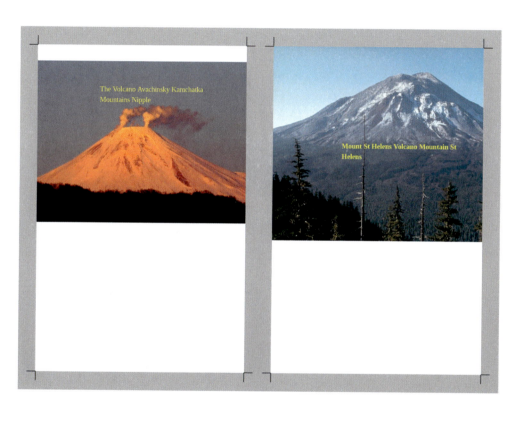

Volcano Eruption Chile

Volcano Zhupanovsky The Eruption
Ash Emission

Sicily Stromboli Volcano Erupts Sea Island Sky

Volcano Klyuchevskaya Sopka The Eruption.

Volcano The Eruption Steam Release Clouds

Volcano Erupting Full Moon Mountain Mt Merapi

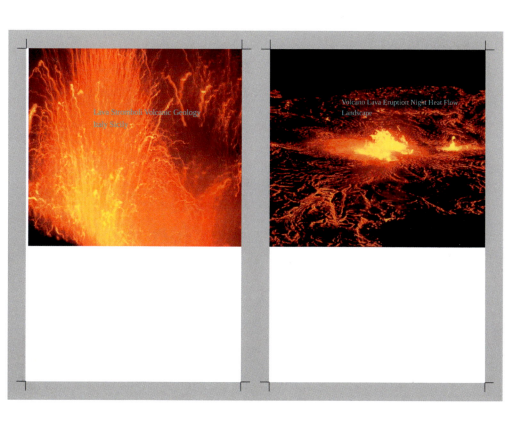

Etna Italy Sicily Landscape Nature Mediterranean

Volcano Japan Kumamoto Aso Morning Glow Asahi

Nature Landscape Eruption
The Volcano Of Capelinhos

Jabal Yemeni Volcano Eruption
Fire Flames Red

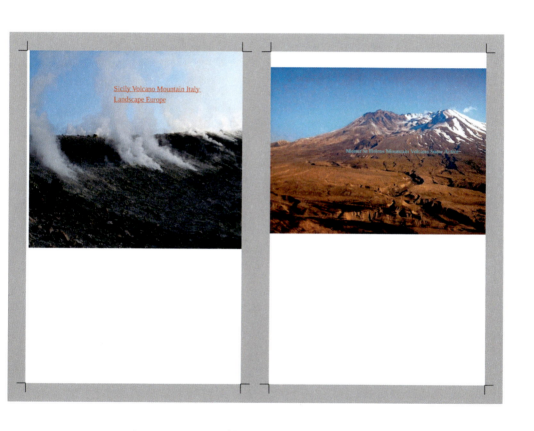

Lava Rocks Volcanic Nature Landscape Travel Sky

Volcano Eruption Chile

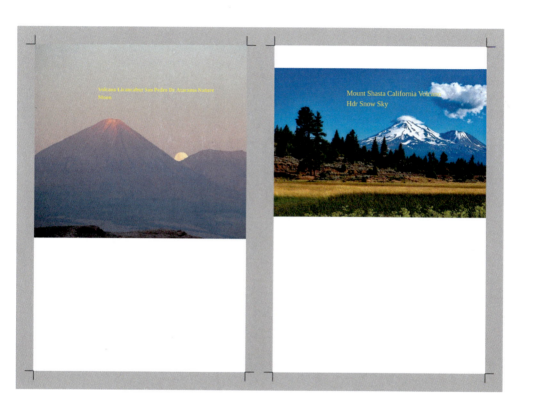

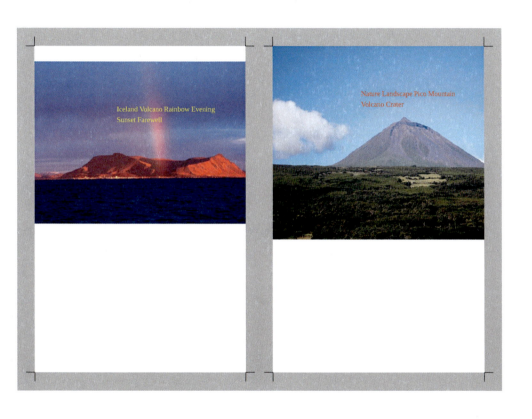

Iceland Volcano Rainbow Evening Sunset Farewell

Nature Landscape Pico Mountain Volcano Crater

Clear Sky Climb Hike Idyllic
Landscape Mountain

Volcano Plant
Landscape

Mountains Volcano The Foot Snow Silt Sastrugi

Mount Shasta California Mountains Volcano Landscape

Climb Cold Daylight Fog Glacier High Hike Ice

Snow Figures Winter Snow Cold Frozen Wind Frost

Volcano Glacier Fumarole Mount Redoubt Alaska Usa

Geyser National Park Wyoming Yellowstone National

New Zealand Hiking Tongariro Sunny Volcano

Volcano Geyser Travel Nature Geothermal Hot Steam

New Zealand Rotorua Zealand Landscape Geothermal

Lanzarote Fire Mountains Volcano Ash Lava

Volcano Eruption Ash Mountain Landscape

Volcano Volcanic Eruption Etna Lava House Shed

Japan Aso Asahi Volcano Sun Kumamoto Light Woods

Mount St Helens Washington Mountains Landscape

Volcano Salt Lake Atacama Desert Desert Dry Chile

Mountains Ridge Volcano Rocks Snow Cornice

Volcano Volcanism Hot Swell Sulfur Iceland

Volcano Clouds Mountains Landscape Indonesia

Ocean Volcano Mountains Wave Sunset Seascape Sea

Volcano Iceland Volcano Krafla Crater Viti Krafla

Snow Winter Frost Coldly Mountains Pass Volcano

Argentina Caviahue Vulcano Ice Lava Nature

Frederic Church Landscape Art Artistic Painting

Crater Lake Iceland Volcanic Crater Volcano Crater

Mountain Merapi Volcano Indonesia Landscape Java

Stromboli Crater Crater Rim Maw Volcano Italy

Hawaii National Parka Volcano Nature Lava Ocean

Hawaii Maui Volcano Crater Horses

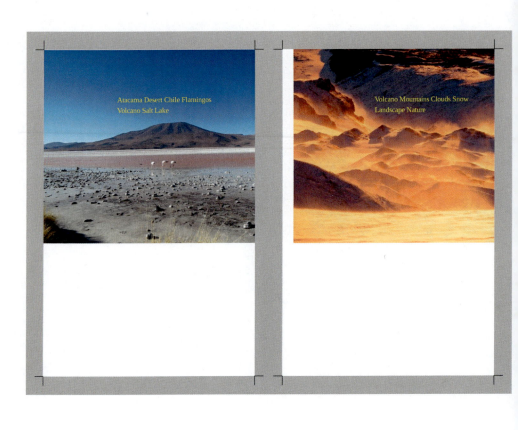

Atacama Desert Chile Flamingos Volcano Salt Lake

Volcano Mountains Clouds Snow Landscape Nature

Haleakala Crater Maui Hawaii Mountain Landscape

New Zealand Volcano Area Rotorua Source Hot Source

Volcanic Crater Volcanic Crater
Crater-Kawa Kerio

Einsturzsee Boulloire eaux brune
Blue Heaven

Mountain Tundra Mountains Ranges Vertices Volcano

Noboribetsu Hell Valley Volcano Japan

Volcano Mount Doom New Zealand
T Tongariro

Snow Winter Snow Cornice Snow Wall
Wave Mountain

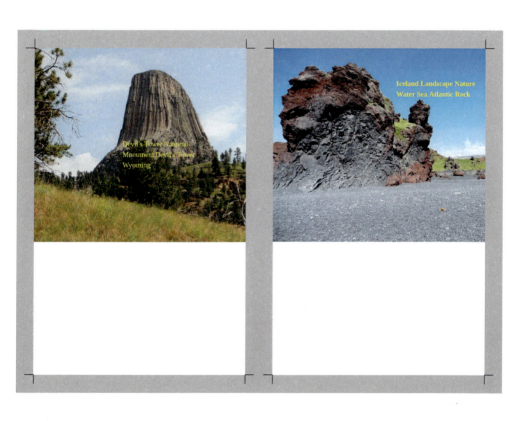

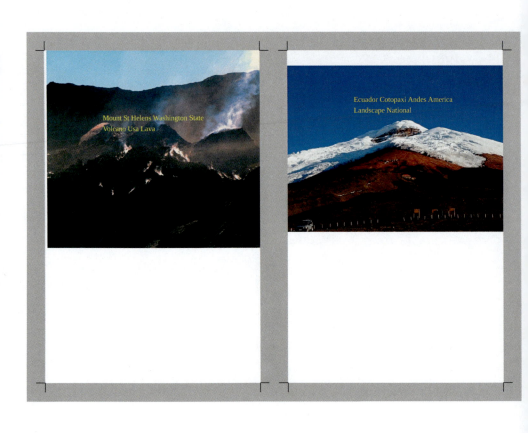

Kilauea Iki Crater Hawaii Hilo
Big Island

Chimborazo Volcano
Ecuador

Crater Volcano Steam

Lanzarote Volcano Crater
Canary Islands

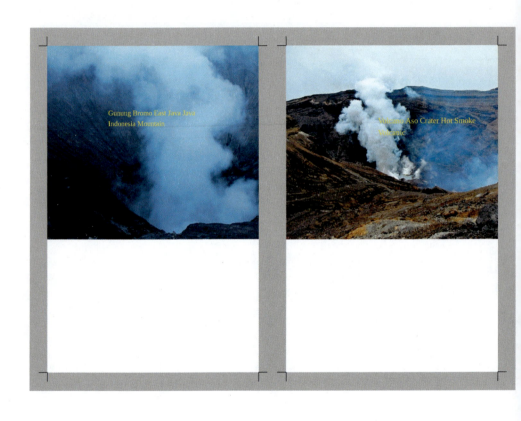

Mountains Place Part Of The Volcano Winter Frost Snow

Yellowstone Water Call Some Volcano

Volcano The Foot Canyon Wind Dust Storm Sand

Hot Source Steam Volcanic Geyser Hot Volcano

Proof

Made in the USA
Monee, IL
19 February 2025

12577478R00064